INTRODUCTION

The richly colored harlequin frogs or stub-toed toads of the genus *Atelopus* are in no way inferior in beauty to the popular poison frogs of the family Dendrobatidae. While numerous publications have appeared on the poison frogs in recent years, the genus *Atelopus* turns up in the literature only sporadically. This imbalance in the hobby literature is likely due to the general perception that *Atelopus* are difficult terrarium charges. According to several specialist authors, *Atelopus* are even "goners" in the terrarium; others, in contrast, attribute high life expectancies to them in the terrarium. So which is correct?

Based on our experiences, harlequin frogs do well in the terrarium when given appropriate care. The bad experiences reported by hobbyists in the early 1980s, particularly with *Atelopus varius* from Costa Rica, had nothing to do with these being short-lived frogs. We had *Atelopus* in our terraria at that time that had arrived together with various poison frogs from a particular exporter from Costa Rica. In this case not only were the *Atelopus* "goners," the dendrobatids were too, because at the time mass importations with bacterial infections arrived here, of which scarcely a specimen had any prospect of surviving. Healthy *Atelopus*, on the other hand, were hardy terrarium animals under appropriate care at the proper temperatures.

Atelopus are diurnal (active

R. D. BARTLETT

Harlequin frogs such as this relatively plain specimen of *Atelopus varius* have proved to be hard, but not impossible, to keep in the terrarium.

during the day), which they can afford to be because, like the poison frogs, they produce highly toxic skin secretions. Such a "poisonous morsel" no doubt permanently cures predators of their taste for "frogs' legs."

We hope with this small volume to be able to make a contribution to the further dissemination of knowledge on the habits and the terrarium keeping of the harlequin frogs. Naturally we are aware that far from all problems of terrarium keeping have been solved. In particular, the breeding of Atelopus is still very problematic. Nevertheless, we are optimistic that progress can be made in this area in the coming years.

For valuable references in the literature and for assistance in the identification of several

Atelopus species, we give our heartfelt thanks to Herman Oostveen (Utrecht, the Netherlands). We also wish to thank Arend van den Nieuwenhuizen (Zevenaar, the Netherlands) and Michael Franzen (Bonn, Germany) as well as Iris Wernli (Wetzikon, Germany) for their support in the preparation of this book.

SOME TAXONOMY

If you examine a harlequin frog, you may be uncertain as to whether you are looking at a frog or a toad. In fact, *Atelopus* are closely related to the true toads and belong to the same family, Bufonidae, and are members of the suborder Procoela (toads, treefrogs, and relatives). The harlequin frogs of the genus *Atelopus* belong to the subfamily

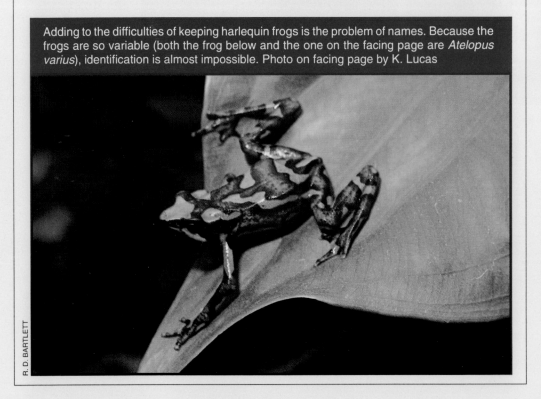

Adding to the difficulties of keeping harlequin frogs is the problem of names. Because the frogs are so variable (both the frog below and the one on the facing page are *Atelopus varius*), identification is almost impossible. Photo on facing page by K. Lucas

R. D. BARTLETT

Atelopodinae. There are about 45 *Atelopus* species, not counting a number of former *Atelopus* species that have been reclassified in the genera *Dendrophryniscus*, *Frostius*, *Melanophryniscus*, and *Osornophryne*. All the herpetologists who have worked with the genus *Atelopus* agree that it is badly in need of revision.

One of the reasons for the necessity of a revision is the diversity of varieties of *Atelopus varius*. This harlequin frog shows itself in a vast variety of forms, which makes identifying the species more difficult.

Some authors, like Savage (1972, *Copeia*), differentiate the *Atelopus* species according to lowland and upland populations and point out anatomical differences in these populations.

According to this view, the most conspicuous differences are in the front feet: lowland populations possess a distinctly longer third toe than do the upland populations. Anatomically, harlequin frogs are distinguished by a slender and bony form. They have a rigid thoracic cage and enlarged processes on the sacral joint. On the basis of this rigid skeleton, the frogs appear to be quite inflexible and awkward. In the majority of species, the innermost fingers and toes are clearly reduced, which has given the animals the common name "stub-toed toads." Because many *Atelopus* exhibit a handsome "harlequin" coloration, this name seems to us to be more appropriate for the attractive frogs.

Facing Page: The brightly colored *Atelopus varius* from Costa Rica are the most familiar harlequin frogs in the hobby as numbers are imported each year. Most, however, do not live long lives in the terrarium. Photo by P. Freed.

Above: Harlequins are in the same family as the true toads, though most are not nearly as warty as the *Bufo atacamensis* from Chile shown here. Photo by R. D. Bartlett.

HARLEQUINS IN NATURE

WHERE DO HARLEQUINS LIVE?

The homeland of the harlequin frogs is extensive areas of Central and South America. The frogs are represented from a latitude of 12° North to 17° South, from Nicaragua in the north to Bolivia in the south. Within this range various species and varieties have formed, some of which have been discovered only recently. Each of these populations also inhabits a specific habitat. Thus, among harlequin frogs there are species that live exclusively in the lowlands and others that may occur in mountains at an altitude of 4000 meters and more.

Shared by all is the preference for a constantly humid tropical climate. For this reason the often exquisitely colored animals are found in the greatest abundance above 1000 meters in the cool

M. SCHMIDT

Searching for *Atelopus* in the Panamanian highlands.

cloud-forest regions of the high mountains. More than 80% of all *Atelopus* live here in the impenetrable tangle of the forest. Characteristic of many *Atelopus* biotopes are small streams with embedded rock formations.

Particularly during the breeding season, hundreds or even thousands of frogs make their way here to attend to the business of mating. These terrestrial frogs live not only on steep riparian slopes, but also on broad plains. Some individuals prefer a rocky substrate, but others live in a thick layer of fallen leaves. We have never found *Atelopus* higher than 20 inches (50 cm) above the ground.

On the basis of information that has been published about the behavior and the living spaces of these frogs, no uniform description of a typical *Atelopus* biotope is possible. Depending on species and range, the requirements for terrarium keeping can vary substantially. This often has been ignored in the care of *Atelopus* in the terrarium,

Facing Page: A colorful burnt orange and brown harlequin frog, probably a variant of *Atelopus varius*. Photo by A. v. d. Nieuwenhuizen.

so that the frogs have unjustly earned the reputation of being short-lived terrarium animals.

OBSERVATIONS IN THE WILD IN PANAMA

We leave the Panamerican Highway to the northeast. Ahead of us lies the massif of Monte Baldo. A crown of dark clouds encircles the more than 3500-meter-high peak of the extinct volcano. The seldom-traveled dirt road gets poorer and poorer, and only slowly do we leave the coastal region of the Pacific side.

A cloud of red dust marks our path, which leads us across extensive parched and treeless landscapes. Meter by meter we wind our way up the mountain. When we reach an elevation of 1000 meters, it is already noticeably cooler and more humid. We approach the tropical cloud forest and pass from the arid lowlands back into lush vegetation. Out of dense clouds of fog suddenly appear the huge trees of the rainforest, covered with the most diverse epiphytes. Meter-wide bromeliads, tillandsias, orchids, ferns, and vines form the impenetrable tangle of this cloud forest. An unearthly feeling accompanies us on our drive through the fog, which reveals only a shadowy representation of our surroundings. With gurgling

One of the several variants of *Atelopus senex* from Volcan Barba. Notice the stubby toes and large webs. Photo by A. v. d. Nieuwenhuizen.

sounds, masses of mud slide down from the steep slopes. More and more frequently, nearly impassable landslides appear from the fog. The temperature is now only 18°C (65°F) at 100% humidity. We hope to find harlequin frogs here. We set up camp at a suitable site. For several days we intend to comb this region for harlequin frogs.

Equipped with our cameras, collecting containers, machete, and compass, we wend our way down a steep ravine. Each step is deliberate. Rotting tree trunks lie as if layered against the fissured, algae-covered cliffs. Not infrequently we slide a few meters downhill before we regain our footing on the slippery ground. Out of the often vertical cliff face

the water trickles down to the valley and enters a small, barely 2-meter-wide stream that materializes before us out of the fog.

Tree trunks and torn-off plant parts wedged between boulders and large rock formations bear witness to the power of the mountain stream, which often swells into a torrent. We travel only a few meters upstream before discovering the first *Atelopus*. On a fallen tree spanning the entire stream perches a full-grown male *Atelopus varius*. Like *Atelopus zeteki*, this species also has bright yellow and black markings, except that the distribution of color is exactly reversed, as with the golden frogs of El Valle.

Totally oblivious to us, the

Keepers must remember that most harlequin frogs (like this *Atelopus varius*) require not only high humidity but also running water to be kept successfully.

R. D. BARTLETT

Atelopus observes its surroundings. After a quick look around it sets out for the opposite bank. After traveling only 20 centimeters, the frog makes its first stop to survey its territory again. With body raised high, the male begins to call. The chirping sound is still audible at a distance of several meters. Soon after, the frog continues on its way, before repeating the same procedure a half meter further on. In this manner the little (about 3.5 cm, 1.4 in) frog slowly disappears into the undergrowth on the other side of the stream. We march upstream through the stream bed. Only sporadically do we discover another frog. So far we have already seen six males, but as yet not a single female.

After we have traveled uphill for several hours, Ralf finds the first pair. With a daring leap that ends with Ralf in the water but the *Atelopus* in the net, we have now also found a female frog from the uplands of the Cordillera Central. With a size equal to that of

R. HESELHAUS

The Golden Harlequin Frog, *Atelopus zeteki*, is no longer available to hobbyists and may be extinct over much of its small range. Many herpetologists consider *zeteki* to be just a local variant of *Atelopus varius* and not recognizable.

Atelopus zeteki, this variety of *Atelopus varius* is one of the largest harlequin frogs.

A few days later we visit the high valley of El Valle, located at an altitude of about 600 meters. Because of its pleasant climate, it is a popular Panamanian resort. We do not visit this valley on account of its curative value, however, but rather because of our interest in the "golden frogs" of El Valle. In the montane forests sur- rounding the valley lives perhaps the most beautiful species of harlequin frog, *Atelopus zeteki*. Unfortunately these frogs have become so rare that they have had to be placed under international protection. *Atelopus zeteki* is listed in Appendix I of CITES as a species threatened with extinction. This protected status means that for *Atelopus zeteki* there is a basic ban in export and trade.

Now we stood in the high valley of El Valle and peered up the mountain slopes: Somewhere up there was where they lived, the last "golden frogs"! Our time was too short for us to be able to search for wild *Atelopus zeteki* so we could photograph them in their natural habitat, but fortunately we had another way to see the golden frogs. We had heard that there was an outdoor terrarium with *Atelopus zeteki* at the Hotel Campestre.

The hotel, set against a dreamlike mountainous backdrop, is surrounded by extensive greenery. At the entrance colorful macaws greet us with their deafening cries. Our attention is drawn, however, to a kind of aviary in the hotel's front garden. Here in this aviary, the bottom third of masonry and enclosed above with wire mesh, is where we in fact discover our first golden frogs. The exquisitely colored frogs come from the mountains in the immediate vicinity, as a bellboy explained to us. These frogs were formerly common; it was even possible to find them in the hotel's garden. Possibly demand from the pharmaceutical industry had contributed substantially to the endangerment of the golden frogs. It is said that a number of years ago large numbers of these harlequin frogs were collected because the pharmaceutical industry was interested in the *Atelopus* skin toxin.

We turn our attention back to the frogs and ask the bellboy if we could photograph the "golden frogs." The bellboy is very helpful and opens the aviary. We now observe the splendid amphibians, which occur in two varieties, at close hand. Besides uniformly orangish gold frogs there are others that exhibit a pattern of black blotches on a golden ground color. The furnishing of the outdoor terrarium consists of several large rocks partially overgrown with mosses and lichens. Various ferns offer the frogs hiding places, and several small pools provide for a high humidity.

After we have photographed the frogs, we take our leave. On leaving El Valle the hope remains that up in the mountains there are still enough golden frogs for them to be able to increase their stocks again. The extinction of these splendid amphibians would be a bitter loss for the Panamanian fauna.

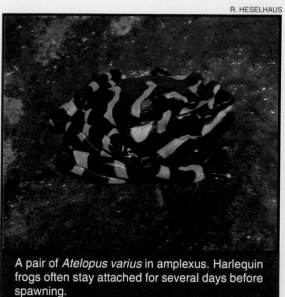

R. HESELHAUS

A pair of *Atelopus varius* in amplexus. Harlequin frogs often stay attached for several days before spawning.

M. PANZELLA

Melanophryniscus stelzneri is a colorful little toad that is closely related to *Atelopus* and often is available to hobbyists. If kept in a roomy terrarium with access to water and small insects as food, it often will live for several years and may even breed.

M. SCHMIDT

Even the cutting of this primitive road through the wilderness of French Guiana may contribute to the destruction of the rainforest.

Facing Page: An interestingly colored harlequin frog, probably a variety of *Atelopus spumarius*. Photo by A. v. d. Nieuwenhuizen.

OBSERVATIONS IN THE WILD IN FRENCH GUIANA

Completely soaked we climb out of our hammocks, which have been our lodgings for several days now. By helicopter we have flown to a region far in the hinterlands of French Guiana in search of the coveted frogs. For more than a week now it has rained throughout the country without interruption, and as we leave our camp in the early morning of our last day it continues to rain.

Although the terrain is not very difficult, the march over the softened and muddy ground takes a lot of energy. Because of the darkness of the primary forest, we luckily encounter only sparse undergrowth, and we can therefore travel unimpeded over the terrain without having to use our machetes. We use only the bush knife for the vital marking of our way. The greatest danger of the jungle is in getting lost. One tree looks like another, one stream like another. It is like a huge labyrinth, and the chance of being found in this green hell is practically zero. Thus with extreme conscientiousness we make our marks every few meters. We also have compasses, which give us an increased feeling of security.

The frogs I found in this region on my last expedition seemingly have been swallowed up by the ground. The raindrops are so big that the frogs have sought shelter from them in their hiding places. Not so the snakes. Only rarely have I seen as many of these reptiles as in the last few days. Besides various small snakes unfamiliar to me, I have also seen poisonous snakes, such as *Bothrops atrox, Bothrops brasili,* and the extremely dangerous Bushmaster. Even a few giant snakes crossed our path. A small (barely 50 cm, 20 in) *Bothrops atrox,* which crept fearlessly out of one of our camera bags, instilled particular respect in us. Caution is absolutely necessary when working in this region!

Unconcerned by the rain, we continue our search until we finally find the first *Atelopus.* As we subsequently learned, it was an *Atelopus spumarius barbatini,* a rather interestingly colored species. The dorsal markings of

R. HEITZ

With lots of patience and a special camera, the authors were able to photograph harlequin frogs in their natural habitat in French Guiana.

the up to 5 cm (2 in) frog consist of numerous intense red squiggles on a black background, which turn to violet toward the belly. The entire ventral side is a uniform violet. These pretty frogs live widely dispersed in hilly terrain, rising to an altitude of 500 meters. The harlequin frogs are not found here in the vicinity of water, but rather about 2 kilometers (1.2 miles) from the nearest stream. Few leaves cover the forest soil forming the living space of this species. Surprising to us is the balanced sex ratio, which is easy to determine by the distinctly larger females.

Following all of the hardships we experienced on this expedition, we are all the more happy over the arrival of the helicopter, which brings us back to civilization in Cayenne.

Our next destination is located not far from the capital. In the car we head for a small chain of hills where I found harlequin frogs on another occasion. The road soon becomes impassable, and we must leave the car. On foot we reach the biotope of *Atelopus flavescens* after about 2 kilometers (1.2 miles). From a distance we can already hear the rattling calls of the males. The frogs (only 4 cm, 1.6 in, long) become more and more abundant the closer we get to a small, slow-flowing stream. The biotope is comparable to a European deciduous forest. A thick layer of large leaves covers the ground, and the roots of the rainforest trees stabilize the sloping banks of the stream. Scattered fallen and rotting tree trunks are among the favorite hiding places of these harlequin frogs. No rocks, no steep slopes, only roots, tree stumps, and the yellowish fallen leaves characterize this biotope, which extends for several kilometers along the stream. In this environment the frogs, which apparently do not range more than 100 meters (330 ft) from their spawning waters, are hard to detect. Virtually ideal is the adaptation to the living space by

M. SCHMIDT

The colors of the French Guiana harlequin *Atelopus spumarius barbatini* are subdued but attractive. Few species of harlequins enter the hobby market on a regular basis.

the beige or orange dorsal coloration of the frogs. Occasionally we find *Atelopus* with yellow dorsal markings, which form a particularly attractive contrast to the often bright violet belly.

Independent of the seasons, *Atelopus flavescens* lives in unchanged abundance in this biotope. The sex ratio is estimated to be 10:1 (males to females), although it must be said that the differences between males and females are not always clear. A concert of calling males accompanies us on our way back to our starting point.

M. SCHMIDT

Atelopus flavescens is usually a brownish harlequin that appears quite undistinguished until you notice the color of the belly.

is one of the most effective toxins in the animal kingdom and, as a rule, spoils the appetite of predators for the otherwise defenseless animals. Since it is disadvantageous for the predator to notice the bad taste of the frogs only after biting them, most harlequin frogs announce their skin toxin with garish colors.

Atelopus contain a strong, dialyzable toxin, atelopidtoxin. The Golden Harlequin Frog, *Atelopus zeteki*, contains particularly large amounts of atelopidtoxin. Among the less poisonous species are *Atelopus varius*, *Atelopus cruciger*, and *Atelopus planispina*. At least with the black, red, and yellow *Atelopus varius* from Costa Rica, the skin toxin, which also contains tetradotoxin, does not provide 100% protection from predators. It has been reported and substantiated with a photograph that the small snake *Leimadophis epinephalus* eats *Atelopus varius* in spite of the skin toxin. This snake apparently has evolved enzymes that make the toxin of the harlequin frogs harmless. In the terrarium, accidents with

SKIN TOXINS AS PROTECTION FROM PREDATORS

For small animals like the harlequin frogs, the struggle for survival is particularly difficult. They must come up with some way to avoid being viewed as an "appetizer" by larger animals. A truly effective protection consists of making oneself unappetizing to predators by developing skin toxins. What does not taste good is not eaten. This survival strategy has been adopted by the harlequin frogs. Their skin toxin

A. V. D. NIEUWENHUIZEN

In a good specimen of *Atelopus flavescens* the entire undersurface is a brilliant pink, sometimes almost violet, in sharp contrast to the brown back and sides.

Atelopus toxin must be avoided. Never handle a harlequin frog if you have cuts on your hands, never put a frog near your eyes, nose, or mouth, and after handling the frogs we should of course wash our hands. The use of *Atelopus* toxin as an arrow poison is unknown.

MASS MATING AT THE SPAWNING WATERS

Like many amphibians, harlequin frogs stage a spectacle at breeding time. By the hundreds, and even the thousands, they gather at their spawning waters to mate.

The highland species among the harlequin frogs breed as a rule in the dry months. Because they live in the ever-wet cloud forests, they need not wait for the rainy season with its temporary bodies of water. It would also be very dangerous for the frogs to breed in the rainy season, because at that time their spawning waters are transformed into raging torrents. Harlequin frogs are poor swimmers and cannot brave strong currents. Furthermore, a torrential mountain stream surely would not be a good nursery for the tadpoles.

In Panama we found *Atelopus varius* at an altitude of about 1400 meters above the Gulf of Chiriqui. In early January the dry season had already lasted for a number of weeks, so that the mass breeding was over in the stream we investigated. We saw only a few stragglers, among them a pair in amplexus.

Though harlequin frogs are toxic, they are relatively harmless to man. Only in the family Dendrobatidae are truly dangerous frogs found, including the deadly Golden Poison Frog, *Phyllobates terribilis*, used by Colombian Indians to tip blowgun darts.

A. NORMAN

R. D. BARTLETT

Among the most beautiful frogs in the terrarium hobby are the poison frogs, such as the Blue Poison Frog, *Dendrobates azureus*, but some of the harlequin frogs can give even these a run for their money.

At the beginning of the dry season, on the other hand, hundreds of *Atelopus varius* gather at this mountain stream. There is a large surplus of males, so they must make every effort to mate one of the clearly larger females. For this purpose males climb to elevated sites within their small territories. With heads raised high, they keep watch from their observation posts so that no ready-to-spawn female escapes their notice. When a spawn-filled female is spotted, they swim and hop to it in order to mount and clasp it. They release their hold only when the mating has led to the desired success and the female has spawned.

The harlequin frog *Atelopus flavescens* from French Guiana is a lowland species that favors the drier months of February to March for breeding. It lives in forested low ground in the immediate vicinity of streams and small rivers. Outside the breeding season we found the frogs rather uniformly distributed on either side of the stream. In an area at a distance of about 20 meters (66 ft) from the water a harlequin frog was noted in about every 4 square meters, but the population density decreased substantially at a distance of 50 meters (165 ft) from the water.

At the beginning of the breeding season the frogs gather

in large numbers on the stream banks. These mass gatherings take place on small steep banks located a maximum of 10 meters (33 ft) from the water. Now up to 50 harlequin frogs can be counted in a square meter. This group consists almost exclusively of males. Arriving females are embraced immediately by the males. As soon as a pair has formed, it leaves the group and goes to the water.

On the bank, in the immediate vicinity of the water's surface, the female then releases her strings of eggs. After that the frogs separate. The female returns to the forest and the male returns to the group.

Because the onset of the rainy season swells the stream only slightly, there is no danger for the spawn and hatching larvae of *Atelopus flavescens* of being washed away by floods. Nevertheless, the first weeks of life are very dangerous for the larvae. Most fall prey to predators, and only a few manage to reach metamorphosis.

The tadpoles of *Atelopus* are adapted to flowing streams and are characterized by short, dumpy bodies, short tails, and large sucking discs on the belly behind the well-developed mouths. They rasp diatoms and other algae from rocks in shallow areas of the stream.

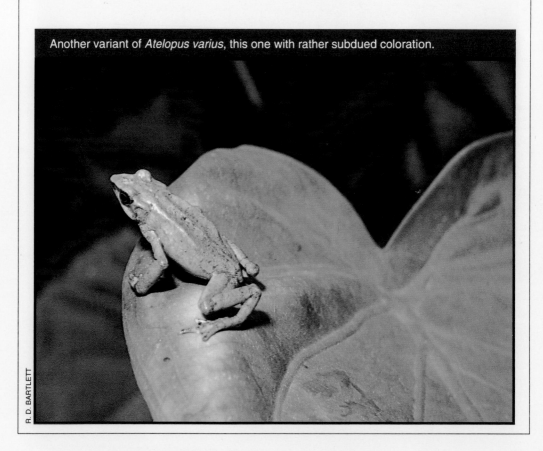

Another variant of *Atelopus varius*, this one with rather subdued coloration.

R. D. BARTLETT

A. V. D. NIEUWENHUIZEN

Above: A froglet of *Atelopus flavescens* just before finishing metamorphosis. **Below:** Aggressive threat posture in *Atelopus flavescens*.

A. V. D. NIEUWENHUIZEN

Atelopus spumarius. Photo by A. v. d. Nieuwenhuizen.

A. V. D. NIEUWENHUIZEN

Atelopus flavescens is quite variable in color. Both these specimens come from Surinam. Often the bright pink belly color is absent, making for a truly dull frog indeed.

A. V. D. NIEUWENHUIZEN

ATELOPUS IN THE TERRARIUM

Many *Atelopus* can be kept for a fairly long period of time only under very specific conditions. Up until just a few years ago, harlequin frogs were considered to be unsuitable terrarium charges. The life expectancy of the frogs rarely exceeded a half a year, and as a rule the amphibians died after a few weeks. Thanks to the efforts of numerous terrarium enthusiasts and new information about the natural habitat, the interesting harlequin frogs now can be described as suitable and long-lived terrarium animals if properly kept. Through use of appropriate keeping methods, the first breeding successes have even been reported.

for harlequin frogs, a height of 40 centimeters (16 in) is sufficient.

During the construction of the silicone-cemented glass terrarium we should give thought to which species we will house in the terrarium. Some *Atelopus* should be kept separated by sex. It is advisable to construct the terrarium from the start in such a way that a divider installed in the middle can compart-mentalize the cage as needed. In this way the sexes can be kept under identical terrarium conditions, yet separately. Simulated seasons also have the same effect on each sex, which is beneficial for breeding attempts. During the breeding season we can remove the divider to bring the frogs together. If necessary, however, we can quickly separate the frogs again.

PHOTO COURTESY OF HAGEN

Standard all-glass aquaria can be used to house harlequin frogs, but it may be necessary to make some changes to accommodate the running stream necessary for most species of the group.

TERRARIA

All *Atelopus* need terraria with the largest possible floor space. As a rule of thumb, 80 X 40 centimeters (32 X 16 in) is the absolute minimum. If the terrarium is to be used exclusively

For the construction of terraria for frogs, there is a wealth of useful guidance in the literature. We have found silicone-cemented

A fitted hood complete with light may be used with harlequins. Be sure the light will support the growth of the plants used in the terrarium.

Terrarium lining can be used in the feeding area to make it easier for the frogs to find their food. Harlequins often appear very clumsy when hunting.

glass terraria to be effective. They are especially easy to service through sliding front panes, but there is no harm in having a good secure lid, especially one with a movable panel and a gauze area. Good ventilation of the terrarium is of particular importance. For this purpose install gauze-covered openings above the front pane and in the rear part of the cover.

The furnishing of the terrarium of course depends on the requirements that the particular species places on the living space. An artificial stream should not be missing from any *Atelopus* terrarium. Only in a well-planned and well-furnished terrarium is there any hope of breeding *Atelopus*. The stream can be installed in many ways. It is of decisive importance that the stream extend over the entire length of the terrarium, to mimic as closely as possible the accustomed flowing water.

As a form for the artificial stream various plastics, such as easy-to-work polyurethane foam or fiberglass-strengthened plastics (polyester or epoxy resins), can be used. With this material the terrarist can let his imagination run free in the shaping of the stream and decoration of the terrarium, so as to also make the terrarium as visually attractive as possible. Rock formations should be installed with cracks and holes present at the height of the water's surface. According to Oostveen (personal communication), *Atelopus* prefer to lay their strings of eggs at these sites during the dry season.

The land section is either formed completely from polyurethane foam or is filled up with peat or orchid root mix. The back and side walls are best covered with cork and orchid root, which makes possible a beautiful growth of ferns and mosses. Rocky structures should not be missing outside of the water either. The frogs like to make their sleeping and hiding places there. The planting should consist mainly of various ferns, mosses, and vines.

CARE AND FEEDING

To make it easier for the frogs to take up food, it is beneficial to leave several open places in the

Like most frogs, *Atelopus* sometimes are active during the day and will need appropriate lighting.

Tight-fitting screen covers may have to be partially covered with glass or plastic in order to increase humidity levels in the terrarium. Harlequin frogs are not great climbers and seldom make dramatic escapes from the terrarium.

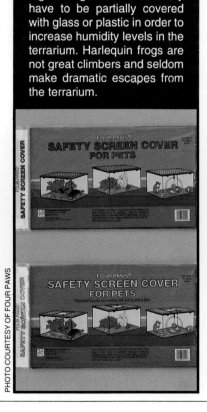

A. V. D. NIEUWENHUIZEN

Snakes and frogs are natural enemies, and the toxic nature of harlequin frogs probably is partially a solution to snake predation.

A community terrarium suitable for *Atelopus*.

M. SCHMIDT

A colorful backing sheet will increase the interest factor of your terrarium. Photo courtesy of Hagen.

MARINA AQUA-DECOR

terrarium. *Atelopus* often hesitate a long time before feeding, so they have great difficulty in catching active food animals on complex surfaces. The location of the *Atelopus* terrarium must also be carefully chosen. A sunny window location absolutely must be avoided, particularly for the highland forms, because the terrarium gets too hot. The ideal location would be a north-facing window in a room that is only moderately heated, even in winter. Newly acquired frogs should be observed closely in the first few weeks. Particularly with *Atelopus* of unknown provenance, the close study of their behavior is necessary to determine their requirements with respect to

Spray vitamins work well with frogs and can be added to the misting water each day.

A good thermometer is necessary for any terrarium.

Submersible aquarium heaters can be used both in the stream running through the harlequin frog tank and in the tank used to hatch the eggs and raise the tadpoles.

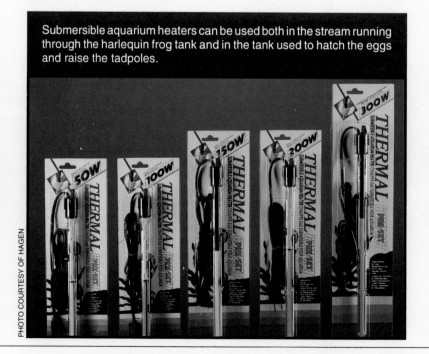

PHOTO COURTESY OF E. G. DANNER

Above: Because you should have running water in the harlequin frog terrarium, you will need a filter to keep the water clean. Use a filter that will work in very shallow water. **Below:** By adapting aquarium pumps and powerheads, you should be able to make a nice little moving water stream across the bottom of the terrarium, but you probably will need advice from your pet shop on the best ways to make the stream.

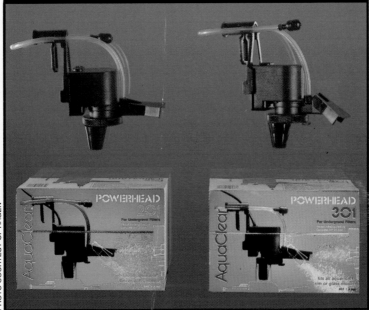

PHOTO COURTESY OF HAGEN

Left: Fruitflies probably are the most certain food for your harlequin frogs because they can be cultivated readily and are cheap to produce. Photo by M. Gilroy.

Below: Don't be afraid to try some more natural foods. Sowbugs, like these *Porcellio scaber*, are abundant and available in a variety of sizes. Tiny young carried under the mother's abdomen might be eaten by even the smallest harlequin frogs. Photo by J. Bateman.

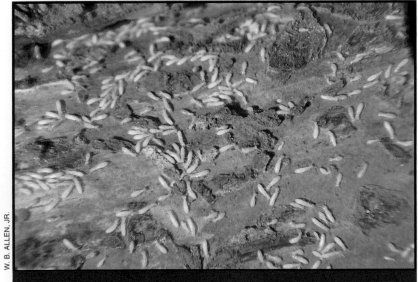

W. B. ALLEN, JR.

In warmer climates termites of various types may be abundant at least seasonally. The typical workers (above) are soft and readily eaten by many small frogs, but the larger soldiers (below) may be a bit dangerous to feed.

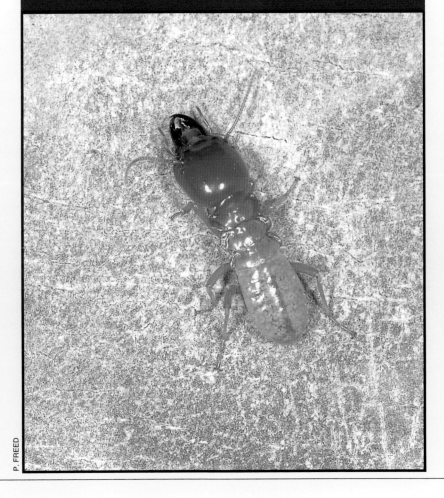

P. FREED

A large variety of plastic plants is available in your local pet shop. Plastic plants can be used to supplement or even replace living plants in many terrarium designs. Photo courtesy of Hagen.

Bromeliads and other epiphytes provide the tropical atmosphere for the harlequin frog terrarium.

temperature, diet, and preferred hiding places. With frogs that refuse to feed during the acclimation phase, it often is helpful to change the temperature in the terrarium.

Some individuals feed at first only when the food animal is held "right in front of their nose." Particularly suitable for this purpose are sluggish waxworms, wax moth larvae. After the acclimation phase, as a rule problems in feeding no longer occur. For a constant food supply the rearing of food animals, such as fruitflies (*Drosophila*), crickets, and wax moths, is recommended.

SOME HARLEQUIN FROG SPECIES

ATELOPUS CHIRIQUIENSIS

Description:

Atelopus chiriquiensis is a medium-sized species. Females reach a length of 36 to 49 millimeters; at 28 to 34 millimeters, the males stay smaller. As a rule *Atelopus chiriquiensis* displays a dark mottling on the back through which the green, yellow, or rusty brown ground color shows. According to Savage (1972, *Herpetologica*), females exhibit variable markings, but males are more uniformly colored. In specimens from Cerro Pando, females are recognizable as a rule by an orange-red dorsolateral stripe. Both sexes have a uniformly yellow belly.

Atelopus chiriquiensis has a moderately long, slightly rounded

Atelopus chiriquiensis from Costa Rica looks much like the Splendid Harlequin Frog but has a wartier skin.

R. D. BARTLETT

A. V. D. NIEUWENHUIZEN

Amplexus in *Atelopus chiriquiensis* may extend over many hours and even days. Because harlequin frogs often are collected in amplexus, both sexes tend to be available on the pet market.

A. V. D. NIEUWENHUIZEN

A. V. D. NIEUWENHUIZEN

Like other harlequin frogs, *Atelopus chiriquiensis* is very variable in color and pattern. Specimens are never as brilliant as many *Atelopus varius*, however.

A. V. D. NIEUWENHUIZEN

Above and Right: The variety of *Atelopus chiriquiensis* shown here (from Costa Rica) has a pattern of fine dark vermiculations on a yellow background color. Notice the relatively long snout and the extent of the webbing on the hind feet. Photos by A. v. d. Nieuwenhuizen.

snout. The skin appears less smooth than in *Atelopus varius*; the fingers and toes have only the rudiments of webbing.

Range and habitat:

Atelopus chiriquiensis inhabits the Atlantic and Pacific mountain slopes in Costa Rica (Cordillera de Talamanca) and in adjoining western Panama (Bocas del Toro, Chiriqui). Its known altitudinal distribution is between 1400 and 1920 meters.

Care in the terrarium:

In the care of *Atelopus chiriquiensis* we must keep in mind that this is a highland species. The terrarium, which should have an area of at least 70 X 40 centimeters, should be unheated and humid, with temperatures between 15°C at night and 22°C during the day. In general, we should keep *Atelopus chiriquiensis* in the same way as the highland forms of *Atelopus varius*.

This mating pair of *Atelopus chiriquiensis* gives an indication of just how variable one population of frogs might be. If you run across this species, remember that it is adapted to Central American highlands and needs fairly cool surroundings like most other harlequin frogs. Photo by A. v. d. Nieuwenhuizen.

ATELOPUS FLAVESCENS

Description:

Atelopus flavescens is a medium-sized harlequin frog that is characterized by its rather oval form. The males often are only slightly smaller than the females, which may be up to 40 mm long. Individuals of different populations scarcely differ in coloration. The dorsal coloration varies from a lemon yellow through orange to dark beige tones. Uniformly colored as well as dark-spotted or mottled forms occur. The belly often is a rich violet, and only a few specimens exhibit a creamy white or brownish underside. The fingers

Atelopus flavescens is relatively constant in coloration and pattern for a harlequin frog, so there is little problem in identification. The feet also are more weakly webbed than in the other common harlequin frogs.

P. FREED

R. D. BARTLETT

This *Atelopus flavescens* is making its way through a jungle of air plants. It prefers warmer temperatures than most common harlequin frogs, making it easier to maintain.

of the front feet are free, and only small rudiments of webbing are present on the toes.

Range and habitat:

Atelopus flavescens occurs predominantly in regions of Surinam and French Guiana near the coast, where the frogs are found between an altitude of 0 and 300 meters. As an exclusive inhabitant of the lowlands, this harlequin frog lives at temperatures of 25 to 28°C in the middle of extensive forests. Characteristic of the biotope is a thick layer of large fallen leaves, many rotting tree stumps, as well as small streams crossing the region. The stream bed consists of a sandy or gravelly substrate. Exposed roots stabilize the bank, which only occasionally exhibits fairly large rock formations.

Care in the terrarium:

As a purely lowland form, this species needs a heated tropical terrarium. The temperatures should be set at 27 to 28°C during the day and 20 to 22°C at night. A small stream provides the necessary humidity and also is a prerequisite for successful breeding attempts. It is essential that this *Atelopus* also be allowed to seek out drier places in the terrarium, which are created by spraying every other day. Several times a year a "rainy season" followed by a "dry period" must be simulated.

Atelopus flavescens is one of the *Atelopus* that has been bred in captivity. Based on a personal communication from Iris Wernli, once a year the frogs attach their clutch in the form of small strings of spawn to the substrate of the stream. The further development takes place in the terrarium. Rearing is difficult because of problems with feeding. The tadpoles feed primarily on algae, which they rasp from vertical surfaces.

The adults can be kept unproblematically in fairly large groups and can also be kept with other terrarium charges. *Atelopus flavescens* is not fussy with respect to diet and also is able to hold its own against other terrarium dwellers.

If it is given a nice stream terrarium, *Atelopus flavescens* survives rather well in captivity and may even breed. Photo by A. v. d. Nieuwenhuizen.

ATELOPUS IGNESCENS

Description:

Atelopus ignescens is without doubt one of the plainest harlequin frogs. The uniformly dark brown, often truly black, dorsal coloration does not resemble in any way the colorful harlequin markings of other *Atelopus*. The black of the back changes to a deep reddish brown toward the flanks, forming a strong contrast to the beige-yellow

R. HESELHAUS

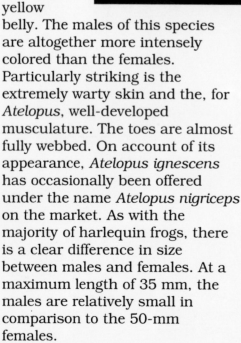

Much wartier than most common harlequin frogs, *Atelopus ignescens* are not colorful animals and would be considered simple toads by many pet keepers.

belly. The males of this species are altogether more intensely colored than the females. Particularly striking is the extremely warty skin and the, for *Atelopus*, well-developed musculature. The toes are almost fully webbed. On account of its appearance, *Atelopus ignescens* has occasionally been offered under the name *Atelopus nigriceps* on the market. As with the majority of harlequin frogs, there is a clear difference in size between males and females. At a maximum length of 35 mm, the males are relatively small in comparison to the 50-mm females.

Range and habitat:

Atelopus ignescens occurs in both Colombia and Ecuador, where it is found, apart from a few Colombian lowland populations, in the high mountain regions at an altitude between 2000 and 4000 meters. Frogs from Ecuador all come from altitudes between 3000 and 4000 meters. The frogs are located in the mountains above Chimbo, at the base of Mount Pichincha; another population occurs at 4000 meters on Mount Chimborazo.

In Colombia there are highly variable areas of occurrence. Near Barbacoa in the Province of Narino, the frogs live at an altitude of only 30 meters, near Guitarilla at 200 meters.

All remaining populations are found between 1300 and 3000 meters in the Province of Cauca near Moscopán (2230 to 2500 meters), the Province of Cordoba above the Rio San Jorge, and in the Province of Narino.

Care in the terrarium:

An unheated terrarium with minimum dimensions of 70 X 40

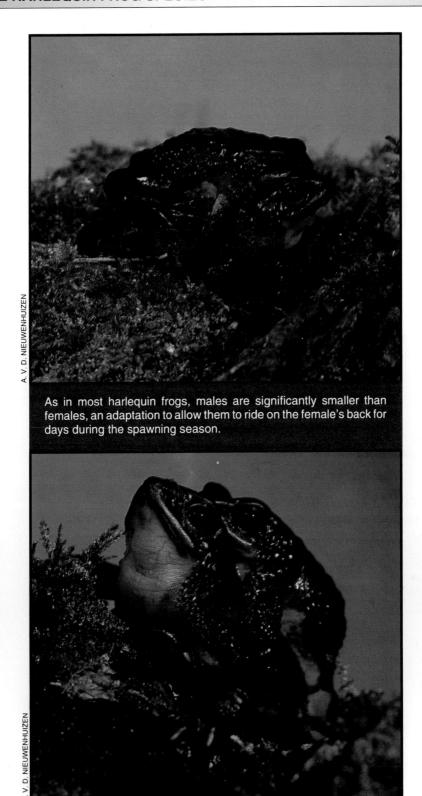

As in most harlequin frogs, males are significantly smaller than females, an adaptation to allow them to ride on the female's back for days during the spawning season.

A. V. D. NIEUWENHUIZEN

A. V. D. NIEUWENHUIZEN

X 40 centimeters is best suited
for the care of the harlequin frog
Atelopus ignescens. Temperatures
during the day in general should
not rise above 20°C and should
fall to 15°C at night. In this
species, the sexes can be kept
unproblematically in groups of
three males and two females. The
males seldom clasp outside the
breeding season. Because
Atelopus ignescens is an
extremely slow eater, it should
not be kept together with other
terrarium animals. Particularly
suitable as terrarium decorations
are stacked shales or other rock
formations that can be covered
with mosses. *Atelopus ignescens*
does not necessarily require
flowing water for breeding.
Should the frogs happen to
spawn, up to 370 eggs can be
expected. With a good diet and
suitable keeping conditions, this
harlequin frog will provide
pleasure for a long time.

As might be expected from the warty skin,
Atelopus ignescens is better protected from
drying out than are other harlequin frogs
and even will breed in standing water.
Photo by A. v. d. Nieuwenhuizen.

ATELOPUS SENEX

Description:

Atelopus senex, described in 1952 by Taylor, is one of the medium-sized harlequin frogs. The males reach a length of 28 to 32 mm. Females, at 43 millimeters, are noticeably larger. The frogs have a very bony build with protruding pelvic bones in the lower back. Also conspicuous is the extensive webbing between the toes, giving the hind legs the appearance of flippers.

The known colorations of Atelopus senex range from a blue-gray to an orange red. Particularly in the flank region, the frogs can exhibit red spots. In contrast to the Atelopus varius varieties, Atelopus senex has a less smooth skin.

Range and habitat:

According to Savage's 1972 review in Herpetologica, Atelopus senex occurs in three regions in central Costa Rica. The species lives on the mountain slopes of the Barba Volcano (1960 to 2040 meters); in the region of Macizo de Cedral, south of San José (2150 meters); and above the Rio Reventazon Basin, south of Cartago (1280 to 1320 meters).

Savage reports on variably colored populations: Specimens from the Barba Volcano are a uniform blue-gray (males) or a uniform rusty red (females). Frogs from the two other localities, on the other hand, do not exhibit a uniform coloration. They can be yellow, greenish yellow, creamy white, or black and may exhibit dorsal markings of spots and bands (Macizo de Cedral). In the region around Navarro on the Rio Reventazon, Atelopus senex appears predominantly black; on the other hand, other populations on the Rio Reventazon are variably colored.

Care in the terrarium:

As a highland species, Atelopus senex needs low temperatures from 18 to 20°C during the day and about 15°C at night. Generally speaking, Atelopus senex has the same requirements in the terrarium as Atelopus varius.

A. V. D. NIEUWENHUIZEN

Atelopus senex shows the very emaciated form typical of many species of harlequin frogs. The skin appears loose on the limbs and the feet are very fully webbed.

Often the colors of *Atelopus senex* appear very mottled, but this is normal and not a disease. Photo by A. v. d. Nieuwenhuizen.

ATELOPUS SPUMARIUS BARBATINI

Description:

At a size of up to 45 mm, the females differ clearly from the up to 35-mm males. The attractively marked frogs exhibit intense red lines or spots on the black or dark-brown ground color. Toward the sides the red changes to a rich violet. The ventral side is uniformly violet, and the throat has dark speckling. The fingers of the front feet are free, and the toes of the hind legs are up to one-third webbed. The skin is smooth.

M. SCHMIDT

Despite their conspicuous coloration, *Atelopus spumarius barbatini* are well camouflaged in their natural habitat.

Range and habitat:

Atelopus spumarius barbatini inhabits the higher-lying regions of French Guiana. In an extensive hilly landscape the frogs live between an altitude of 300 and 600 meters on the floor of the primary forest. This harlequin frog, like *Atelopus varius*, is dependent on bodies of water only during the breeding season. During the rainy season *Atelopus spumarius barbatini* withdraws into its territory, which at times is located several kilometers from the nearest stream.

The frogs live here widely scattered, but in a balanced sex ratio. The biotope, despite the frequent and heavy rainfall, is relatively arid. *Atelopus spumarius barbatini* is sedentary and makes its hiding places among the roots of large trees and in the leaf litter. Twice a year *Atelopus spumarius barbatini* returns to its spawning waters to breed. Small (up to 1.5 meters wide), shallow streams are the destination of the migration.

Care in the terrarium:

Atelopus spumarius barbatini is an undemanding and hardy terrarium charge. At temperatures of 23 to 26°C during the day and 20°C at night, this harlequin frog can also be kept successfully with other frogs. The mutual care of both sexes presents no problems. Only during the breeding season do the males clasp the females for a short time. *Atelopus spumarius barbatini* is not very fussy with respect to diet. A prerequisite for breeding attempts is a terrarium with a large ground area and a well-isolated stream, the water level of which can be varied.

ATELOPUS SPUMARIUS SPUMARIUS

Description:
This small, attractively colored *Atelopus* grows to a maximum length of 35 mm in females, males reaching a length of 30 mm. On a slightly granulated skin, *Atelopus spumarius spumarius* shows a yellow ground color that is broken up by fine black netting on the back and merges to a creamy white toward the flanks. The throat is white, the belly pale yellow. Particularly attractive are the bright red feet. The fingers are free and the toes are half webbed.

Range and habitat:
Atelopus spumarius spumarius inhabits the cloud forest region of the Cordillera Azul (East Andes) in Peru. It lives there between 1300 and 1800 meters along small streams and in the adjoining undergrowth of the steep mountain slopes. The harlequin frogs make their hiding places in

M. SCHMIDT

Rear view of *Atelopus spumarius spumarius.*

M. SCHMIDT

The attractively colored *Atelopus spumarius spumarius* reacts sensitively to high temperatures in the terrarium.

the mossy undergrowth. This region is characterized by constantly high humidity.

Care in the terrarium:
In the terrarium *Atelopus spumarius spumarius* should be kept at temperatures from 18 to 23°C. The harlequin frog tolerates higher temperatures only for a short time. A constantly high humidity is of decisive importance for the well-being of the frogs. The terrarium can be very thickly planted, because this *Atelopus* stays not only on the bottom, but rather is also found in the higher parts of the terrarium. The frogs

have no difficulty in food intake and even manage food animals that would be too large for much more robust *Atelopus*. The sluggish caterpillars of the small wax moth, which should be fortified regularly with vitamins and calcium, are particularly suitable food animals. Keeping the two sexes together is possible only under certain circumstances. As a rule, the males clasp for only a few days and then release the females again. Nevertheless, the keeper should then pay close attention so as to be able to separate the frogs if necessary. In the community terrarium, *Atelopus spumarius spumarius* is displayed to best effect only when it is not dominated by larger terrarium inhabitants.

This *Atelopus* seems to have a snout shaped like *A. spumarius spumarius*, but the pattern is much more simplified. It probably represents an individual variant of that species. Photo by A. v. d. Nieuwenhuizen.

SPLENDID & GOLDEN HARLEQUINS

ATELOPUS VARIUS VARIUS, SPLENDID HARLEQUIN FROG

The classification of *Atelopus varius* into subspecies and color varieties presents a major scientific problem. Keferstein in 1867 described the red and/or yellow and black frogs from Costa Rica as *Atelopus varius.* Subspecies were erected for Costa Rican *Atelopus* by Taylor in 1952, who described, besides *Atelopus varius varius, Atelopus varius loomisi* and *Atelopus varius ambulatorius.*

Additional subspecies live in Ecuador *(Atelopus varius elegans),* in Colombia *(Atelopus varius subornatus, Atelopus varius*

bibroni), and in Panama (Darien, *Atelopus varius glyphus).* Savage, in his 1972 review, recognizes no subspecies for *Atelopus varius* from Costa Rica and western Panama; he considers all *varius* forms there to be the nominate form. We follow Taylor and will designate all Costa Rican *Atelopus varius* as *v. varius;* only *Atelopus varius loomisi* and *Atelopus varius ambulatorius* are kept separate. For valuable information on localities, we give our heartfelt thanks here to Herman Oostveen (Utrecht).

Description:

The Splendid Harlequin Frog is one of the most striking species of *Atelopus.* The frogs often exhibit a gorgeous harlequin coloration consisting of red, yellow, green, blue, white, and black markings. The range in colors and forms is so great that a uniform description of the species is impossible. The males remain smaller than the females; both sexes produce chirping calls.

In the following pages we would like to discuss several populations and subspecies so that at least a geographic classification will be possible with these frogs. When

The bright black and yellow coloration of a typical Costa Rican Splendid Harlequin Frog, *Atelopus varius*, is hard to surpass. Many specimens also have touches of red and blue on the back. Photos by A. v. d. Nieuwenhuizen.

the locality is known, an indication of the required conditions in the terrarium is then at least possible.

Range and habitat:
A very small form of the Splendid Harlequin Frog comes from the central mountains around the city of San José, Costa Rica. Here the females reach 40 mm in length and the males 30 mm. These frogs are predominantly red and black on the dorsal side with only small yellow to cream-colored spots. Pure red and black specimens without yellow markings also occur. The light yellow to cream-colored belly stands in contrast to the dark dorsal side. This form of *Atelopus varius varius* inhabits moist mountain slopes at an altitude of 1100 and 1600 meters.

Another population of *Atelopus varius varius* lives in the Monteverde Cloud Forest Reserve in Costa Rica. The heart of the reserve lies at altitudes between 1450 and 1850 meters. On average, 2430 millimeters of precipitation falls here annually: October is the month with the highest rainfall, February and March are the driest months. The average temperature is 19°C, although the range is between 12 and 27°C.

Some parts of the reserve—on account of fog and regular rainfall—can be designated as ever-wet cloud forest. The constant high humidity promotes the growth of mosses, ferns, bromeliads, and orchids.

Atelopus v. varius occurs in this region in an amazing range of forms. The most abundant color form is individuals that exhibit a coarse yellow, green, or yellow-green pattern on a black ground color. These frogs were exclusively females, as were rarer individuals with a fine yellow netting. In the males, it was not possible to detect a color scheme: each specimen was different! The spectrum here ranges from uniformly black frogs to bluish yellow mottled individuals. The markings of the males are considerably more diffuse and less clearly defined than are those of the females.

In our experience and in the experience of other authors, an absolute prerequisite for an "*Atelopus varius* biotope" is a small, fast-flowing stream or river with rock formations and thick vegetation on the banks.

Care in the terrarium:
Terraria starting at a minimum size of 80 X 40 X 60 centimeters (length X width X height) are suitable for the care of *Atelopus varius*. Because the frogs do not climb much, the ground area should be as large as possible. This also is necessary for the installation of the "stream," which should not be missing from any *Atelopus varius* terrarium. Suitable as a substrate are slabs of peat with root fibrils, which we layer such that they rise toward the back. Through the planting of ferns, mosses, climbing plants, and bromeliads, we can create a vegetation-rich "stream bank."

In the foreground we should install a "stream" a few

centimeters deep with a filter pump. In the aquatic section we put several smooth, flat rocks in part covered with water and in part projecting above the water's surface to provide perches and lookout posts for the harlequin frogs. A high humidity between 80 and 100% is achieved by humidity from the aquatic section, through the constantly moist peat, and through the daily spraying of water.

The air and water temperature must not be too high for *Atelopus varius varius*. During the day we keep the frogs at temperatures between 18 and 22°C, with nocturnal cooling to about 15°C.

These harlequin frogs feed on small insects and spiders. In addition to fruitflies (*Drosophila*), young crickets, wax moth caterpillars, and "meadow plankton" can be fed. Because *Atelopus* are rather deliberate animals, we should mainly offer them sluggish insects like wax moth larvae. A dusting of the food animals with a calcium and vitamin preparation is recommended for maintaining vitality.

The breeding of *Atelopus varius* unfortunately has succeeded only partially so far. For Kneller (personal communication), the frogs spawned in a greenhouse. The larvae were reared, but died for unexplained reasons before the metamorphosis.

Jungfer (1988, *Herpetofauna*) reports on the rearing of *Atelopus varius* tadpoles that he brought back from Panama. He found the black larvae with whitish yellow spots in a tributary stream of the Rio Hornito on the downstream side of vertical surfaces of boulders. Jungfer mentions that, like other tadpoles from flowing water, they have very small tails that exactly equal the length of the body. With the aid of the unique sucking disc just behind the lower lip that covers almost the entire belly, the tadpoles can attach themselves firmly to rocks. Jungfer reared the tadpoles with algae, which they always grazed from vertical surfaces. After the metamorphosis the greenish gray juveniles were 7 millimeters long. At first they fed on springtails, later *Drosophila.*

In laboratory experiments, a female *Atelopus varius* laid 950 eggs in several strings. The individual egg was 1 millimeter in diameter, and the developmental period until the hatching of the larvae was six days. In the wild, *Atelopus varius* pairs are said to stay in amplexus for up to 19 days before they spawn. Keeping *Atelopus varius* separated by sex has been recommended. This seems reasonable, because the sight of a female is a signal for the male to clasp. The males clasp so tightly that females not yet ready to spawn can be strangled. When the females do not spawn, there is the danger that the males will starve, since they do not feed during amplexus. The male does not loosen his grip until the female has laid her strings of eggs.

In the wild the females are found near the males only during the breeding season. The males occupy small territories along the river, where they are found all year. The females, on the other hand, withdraw into the adjoining forest following the breeding season.

For breeding, the frogs should be put together in an aquarium filled with about 15 cm of water and with strong water movement (a simulated stream). Fairly large stream stones should be put in the water and should project partially above the water's surface. Because *Atelopus varius* lays its strings of spawn in wet rock crevices, we do not think it necessary to introduce aquatic plants. To what extent the regular breeding of *Atelopus varius* in the terrarium can be realized, we will not venture to guess at the moment. Whether harlequin frogs as "traditional spawners" spawn only in the river of their birth, as has been suggested, seems doubtful to us. With the increased knowledge of the reproductive biology of harlequin frogs, it could be possible to propagate these attractive amphibians continuously.

The simple pattern on the back marks the weak subspecies *Atelopus varius ambulatorius* from Isla Bonita, Costa Rica.

ATELOPUS VARIUS AMBULATORIUS

Description:

With a length of 33 mm, *Atelopus varius ambulatorius* is one of the smallest forms of the *varius* group. This subspecies differs from the nominate form and from *Atelopus varius loomisi* through the absence of any shades of red. In addition to the lemon-yellow, black-marked dorsal surface, this delicate harlequin frog displays a creamy white to pale yellow belly that features a few blue-black marks. Webbing is absent from the fingers, but the toes are up to two-thirds webbed. The head is more pointed than in *Atelopus varius loomisi.*

Range and habitat:

Atelopus varius ambulatorius occurs in Costa Rica (Isla Bonita) on the southeastern slopes of the Poás Volcano at an altitude of about 2000 meters. Taylor found this subspecies sleeping at night on a large leaf in the vicinity of a small river. According to Taylor, *Atelopus varius ambulatorius* and *Atelopus varius loomisi,* both of which occur in the Isla Bonita region, differ in that they occur at different altitudes. Only the first subspecies ranges up to an altitude of 2000 meters. (Ed. note: The occurrence of two "subspecies" is this limited area is biologically unlikely. Readers should note that these names have been considered synonyms of typical *varius* by most herpetologists who have investigated the situation. They may represent small populations with slightly variant color patterns that perhaps may not be constant over the course of several years.)

Care in the terrarium:

Because *Atelopus varius ambulatorius* is a purely montane form, this subspecies should be kept somewhat cooler than the previously described highland forms of *Atelopus varius varius*. The daytime temperature should not exceed 20°C, and the temperature should drop to about 15°C at night.

ATELOPUS ZETEKI, GOLDEN HARLEQUIN FROG

Description:

This gorgeously colored *Atelopus* species is unfortunately threatened with extinction and therefore is listed in Appendix I of CITES. The "golden frogs" may neither be imported nor exported, and therefore are unavailable to hobbyists. For the sake of completeness, however, we will include a brief presentation of this species.

Atelopus zeteki reaches a length of 55 mm and is therefore one of the largest harlequin frogs. Besides uniformly golden yellow individuals, there are others that display a pattern of black spots on a golden yellow ground color. *Atelopus zeteki* has an attractive yellow-green iris and a head elongated into a snout with a slightly overhanging "nose." It has virtually no webbing on the fingers and toes.

Range and habitat:

The Golden Harlequin Frogs live in the high valley of El Valle not far from Panama City. They are found at altitudes between 600 and 1000 meters. Unfortunately, the frogs are today found only in inaccessible mountain gorges; formerly they ranged down into the valley. Ong (1983, *DATZ*) found the golden frogs in a fast-flowing mountain stream about 3 to 6 m wide. The stream bed was rocky and largely free of vegetation, and the water had a temperature of 21°C. The banks were covered with bushes and trees. *Atelopus zeteki* perches on rocks in the river in full sunlight. The frogs are not wary and apparently rely on their skin toxin to prevent predation.

A. KERSTITCH

A pair of Golden Harlequin Frogs, *Atelopus zeteki*, in amplexus.

A. V. D. NIEUWENHUIZEN

Atelopus cruciger of Venezuela is one of many harlequin frog species that occasionally appear in the pet trade but seldom survive long except in the hands of an expert.